Clothing Brand Playbook: The Ultimate Step-By-Step Guide on How to Start and Grow a Clothing Brand

By Yaswanth Nukasani

Idea & Planning | Garment Blanks | Graphic Design | Getting Your Apparel Printed | Packaging Options | Get Started

Clothing Brand Playbook:
The Ultimate Step-By-Step Guide on How to Start and Grow a Clothing Brand
Yaswanth Nukasani

Written By Yaswanth Nukasani ©
www.yaswanthnukasani.com

ACKNOWLEDGEMENTS

As I write this, there is this quote that comes to mind, "Life is about We. Not Me." Indeed! Looking back, it is crazy to see that the blessings in our lives are often in some part due to the help, support, and sacrifices of others. This is especially true in my case.

It is literally impossible to list out all the people on one page who have helped me along the way, that would be a book in itself. I thank you from the bottom of my heart, and you know who you are.

Although this list is far from complete, I wouldn't be where I am today if it was not for these people:

- To Christ, who loves me recklessly, who gave me the answer to all my heart's questions and troubles, who built a fort around me during the hard and good times and who gives me this abundant blessed and driven life which I live today.

> *13 I can do all things through Christ who*
> *strengthens me.*
> *~ Philippians 4:13*

- To my mom and dad, who bravely left everything they knew in search of a better life here in the United States for my sister and me, who have also supported me with their words, sacrifices, resources, and love consistently over the last 22 years.

Written By Yaswanth Nukasani ©
www.yaswanthnukasani.com

- To my sister, who likes me for me and is not impressed by any accomplishments, success, etc..

- To my grandparents, cousins, and their families, uncles, and extended family.

- To my friends, mentors & supporters, who give me strength through the hard times.

- Fellow entrepreneurs and business owners, who remind me that anything indeed is possible and give me a supporting hand.

To the countless number of un-mentioned people who changed the trajectory of my life for the better, without me being aware of it...

Written By Yaswanth Nukasani ©
www.yaswanthnukasani.com

INDEED… as the saying goes, "it takes a village to raise a child".

Meet The Author

Hey there! Thanks for trusting me and picking up this book. Before you get started on this book and journey, I wanted to share my story, so there is context to what you are about to read. My name is Yaswanth Nukasani, and at the time I am writing this book, I am a 22 years old college student. My whole life, I have always been involved in some entrepreneurial ventures in different capacities. My family and I moved to the United States when I was in the 3rd grade. Due to the blessings of this country, I have had many opportunities from a young age to learn, seek mentorship, and grow as an aspiring entrepreneur. I started my clothing line 6 years ago when I was in high school with one of my best friends, Matt. We started the Phi Concept! We knew nothing about the clothing business and even how to get a shirt made to sell. However, being of a curious mind, we spent a lot of time trying to find the answers. Years and years of learning, making mistakes, making changes, but continuously growing and learning. We were and are still young, so we have time on our side. My mission behind writing this book is because I wanted to share what I have learned in a practical and actionable manner over the years with all aspiring fashion entrepreneurs who want to start their own clothing brand!

Today, our brand is still young, and we are still growing. Along with the Phi Concept, I have built other ventures, some in the clothing industry such as Merchn.com and ones like Once Upon a Brick Land Investments in the real estate space.

I believe each venture or entrepreneurial leap we take is a stepping stone to the next version of ourselves and our entrepreneurial careers.

Somewhere along the lines, I fell in love with the process. Today, I work on growing my companies and sharing what I learn with others without holding back any "secrets" as I believe in cultivating an abundant state of mind.

I hope this book adds value to your life and inspires you to live a prolific and abundant life in all areas.

Let's Get Started.

Written By Yaswanth Nukasani ©
www.yaswanthnukasani.com

TABLE OF CONTENTS

| Coming Up with the Idea of Your Brand | Garment Blanks | Design| Decoration Methods | Packaging Options | Marketing | Numbers

CHAPTER: The Idea and the Plan for Your Brand

Coming Up with the Idea

Before we dive into the nitty-gritty details of how to get shirts printed, how to work with designers, and all that fun stuff, it is helpful to have somewhat of a clear idea of what your brand is or what you want your brand to be and become. If you already have this idea, skip the next couple of pages...

Remember, a brand is a lot different than one design. If you have one amazing t-shirt design idea, that's great! However, as a brand, I would hope that you plan to put out a series of designs over an extended period of time. 1, 5, 10 years and so on.. Something which lasts the test of time.

What does your brand stand for? Who do you see wearing your brand? Even things like what "vibe" / style?

"brand persona" is something you can dive into to crystallize what you are trying to express as a designer and a clothing brand.

Weebly put out a great article on, "what is a brand persona?"

> *A brand persona is a collection of personality traits, attitudes, and values that your brand showcases on a regular basis to help connect with a certain audience segment. A brand persona can be a person, character, mascot, or idea.*

> *"The purpose of personas is to create reliable and realistic representations of your key audience segments for reference. These representations should be based on qualitative and some quantitative user research and web analytics," according to usability.gov.*

A good brand persona is one that you can almost visualize as someone you know. You can also think of it as a mirror image of yourself when interacting with the brand. As a small business creating a brand persona, the easiest way to create a personality for your company is to envision the type of person you think would be most interested in our products and services and create messaging for them. Think of a brand persona as the "character" that best represents what you are about, such as the owl for Wide Eyed Cold Brew.

An authentic persona can help establish trust with users and help maintain their loyalty. This is especially good for eCommerce websites, as an effective persona can positively impact sales. <u>What is a Brand Persona, and Why Do I Need One?</u>

Once you have formed the "character" of your brand, another thing to think of or tap into is your *brand story...*

Every brand pretty much always has some form of a story.

What made YOU want to create your brand and put it out into the universe? You could have totally just found some cool brand online, purchased the clothing, and wore it. If you are reading this, there is something in you that wants to create or express. An idea, a message, a style, a vibe, etc. whatever it is.. Something which you want to share.

The story can be but not limited to,

How did you come up with the idea of starting your brand? What made you want to take the risk? There are 1000s of brands out there. What do you think is going to make your brand remarkable or needed?

Is it a certain type of color-way? A "look"?

Maybe it was an event which might have happened in your life or something you experienced

Whatever it is... It is always helpful to write down the clear vision and idea of your brand so it can be clearly communicated to your customer base.

The following two things can be a good starting point for you to explore the nature of your brand and help you form it.

Vision Statement

A vision statement is a declaration of an organization's objectives, intended to guide its internal decision-making.

Written By Yaswanth Nukasani ©
www.yaswanthnukasani.com

A vision statement usually is one-sentence. It often expresses what it is you are trying to accomplish 10, 20, 30 years, etc. from now. A long-term goal.

Here are some examples which I found inspiring from the non-profit sector:

- Goodwill: Every person has the opportunity to achieve his/her fullest potential and participate in and contribute to all aspects of life. (21)
- charity: water believes that we can end the water crisis in our lifetime by ensuring that every person on the planet has access to life's most basic need — clean drinking water.
- Habitat for Humanity: A world where everyone has a decent place to live. (10)
- Creative Commons: Nothing less than realizing the full potential of the Internet — universal access to research and education, full participation in culture — to drive a new era of development, growth, and productivity. (30)

Written By Yaswanth Nukasani ©
www.yaswanthnukasani.com

https://topnonprofits.com/examples/vision-statements/

When we look at the clothing/fashion sector, here are some famous examples:

- Patagonia: Build the best product, cause no unnecessary harm, use business to inspire and implement solutions to the environmental crisis.
- Life is Good: To spread the power of optimism.
- Warby Parker: To offer designer eyewear at a revolutionary price while leading the way for socially conscious businesses.

https://blog.hubspot.com/marketing/inspiring-company-mission-statements

Mission Statement

According to Chris Bart, professor of strategy and governance at McMaster University, a commercial mission statement consists of three essential components:

- Key market: the target audience.
- Contribution: the product or service.
- Distinction: what makes the product unique or why the audience should buy it over another.

Why do you really want to do this? What are you setting out to do? What is the purpose of you guys existing?

So having an understanding of both of those can be very compelling. And I think it's a great place to start to understand your brand and what it is that you're trying to do a little bit better.

Now that you are starting to think of some of these things in addressing your brand, let's hop into something even more exciting, picking the garments for you to bring to life with your brand!

Three Steps to Get Started

Set Goals

To set up your goals, you should use the S.M.A.R.T formula that implies five characteristics:

- Specific– Be as explicit as you can because the more precise you are, the better the results.

- Measurable – When you set a specific goal, you can measure it. You should be able to answer "How Much?" "How Many?" and "By When?"

- Attainable –This means that your goals should be realistic while relying on the resources that are at your disposal. That will guarantee you will reach them and that you are not just nurturing false expectations.

- Relevant– Your goals also need to help you reach your visions. You can see that those two are well connected. Without a vision, you can't develop goals, and without reaching your goals, you can't accomplish your vision.

- Timely– What is the deadline for each goal? If you don't set up the period you are supposed to complete something, you won't be able to measure them, therefore, neither to reach them.

Set up your budget

This is a very important step. You need to create your budget. That includes calculations such as the costs of launching your clothing line and the costs of making your business sustainable.

How much are you going to spend on the packaging or creating your product?
What fabrics are cost-efficient?

If you are planning to build an e-commerce website, you need to include the costs that come with it, too.

There are multiple ways to cut your costs at the beginning, but make sure that you always provide the quality and value as in that way, your efforts will pay off.

When I was starting my clothing line, the Phi Concept, we have set our budget to be $1000. At the minimum, a budget between $500-$1000 will be good for you. If you create a budget, stick to it. Many people blow their money fast and often don't think about having some operating capital in the bank.

3. Create a Business Plan

When you are developing your own brand, it is helpful to have a marketing strategy and a budget.

The only thing left is to put all the pieces together. Write everything down on a piece of paper and create a business plan

This will help you have clarity on your business. It also helps with your ability to be consistent.

Having everything in one document will help you have the whole picture of your business on one page.

Human brains are not capable of holding all the information perfectly, so it is good to write it down.

This plan is extremely important to have, but also being able to adapt to any market changes is just as important.

However, nothing is as important as taking action. There is a famous quote by Mike Tyson, "Everyone has a plan until they get punched in the face."

Let's Get Started...

Garment Blanks

So you have thought about the idea for your brand, and now you want to put out your first design…

Well, you need to start with what is commonly referred to as the "blank" or the "garment."

A "blank," as the name implies, is a blank garment which has no designs or imprint.

This is the actual blank t-shirt, hoodie, hat, long sleeve tee, etc. that you will be printing on or "decorating" to have a product to sell.

Usually, there are two options, you can either use "pre-made" blanks, or you can start from scratch and "cut & sew" and build your garment from the group up.

Pre-made blanks are basically clothing companies like American Apparel, Bella + Canvas, Gildan, etc. who manufacture a wide variety of clothing without any kind of design on it. They basically make blank t-shirts, hats, hoodies, etc. so that you can print/decorate them with your own designs/logo.

The benefit of this is you can buy very low minimum quantities as many or as little as you want. You also don't have to order in high quantities, work with factories, source fabric, and everything which goes into producing apparel.

I believe that for a new brand that is starting in their streetwear brand journey, pre-made blanks are a great way to find your proof of concept.

I have included a supplier list of wholesalers in the next few pages where you can start shopping for your blank garments and view your options

---

First Quality, Graded Irregulars & Mill Graded

In blank apparel, there are a few levels of quality or types of garments. The safest, most reliable, and the industry-standard is First Quality Merchandise.

⇨ First Quality Merchandise

First Quality Merchandise is a retail-ready product that comes straight from the factory. The t-shirt etc. has gone through the manufacturer's Quality Control standard, and only if it passed will it make its way to the wholesaler for you to purchase.

Suppliers S&S Activewear, AlphaBroder, etc. will usually only deal with first-quality. There are many benefits that you gain from working with First quality merchandise. The main ones are consistency. You can expect the suppliers to usually have the garment in all sizes, colors in stock when you sell out of your first batch of tees, etc. to re-order so you can sell more!

After First Quality Merchandise, there are a few other categories that exist.

One of our suppliers has provided a great explanation of the rest of the quality levels and breakdown of some of the major categories:

⇗ *Closeouts/Overstocks (Higher Quality)*

This category contains clothing known as closeouts, excess inventories, overstock, discontinued, etc., that are all flawless, first quality merchandise. *First quality apparel originally made for retail channels may still have their original branded hangtags and/or UPC stickers just as you would find them in a department store.*

Closeouts or first quality clothing created for the printable, screenprinting, or embroidery industries will often come without branded ticketing or tags depending on the manufacturer, and/or which stage of their production they were decidedly `closed out". Private label closeout apparel may include clothing with brand *labels that have been removed or left off; these closeouts will still have care, content, and/or size label. Closeouts can also be stock lots or canceled production orders. These are the highest quality off-price clothes available.*

Closeout Customers: *Mass Market Retail Chains, Screen Printers, Promotional*
Businesses, Resort Wear Stores

⇨ Graded Irregulars *(Medium Quality)*

This category contains clothing considered non-first quality or slightly irregular by the manufacturers. This can be for a multitude of reasons including, but not limited to, fabric defect, construction imperfections, slight dye lot discrepancies, or slight sizing issues. However, our staff looks through each and every piece to inspect for visible flaws. Those with major visible flaws are dropped into the (*3rds*) category below. Those without major noticeable are sold as a very clean, or as we call it, hand graded irregular. The primary difference between these and first quality garments are the marked, clipped, or stamped labels behind the neck. Also, hand graded irregular clothing will typically not have any retail hang tags or UPC adhesives.

Graded Irregular Customers: *Discount Retail Chains, Variety & General Merchandise Stores, Hospitals, Screen Printers*

⇨ Mill Graded Irregulars (LOWEST Quality)

This category contains clothing considered non-first quality or slightly irregular by the manufacturers. *Again, this can be for a multitude of reasons including, but not limited to, fabric defect, construction imperfections, slight dye lot discrepancies, or slight sizing issues. RG Riley has not culled, graded, or looked through these garments. They are sold exactly as they arrived and may contain some visible flaws. In some cases, you may find a sticker, tape, or flag near the irregularity marking its location. Mill Graded Irregulars or Clothing Seconds will vary in quality from manufacturer to manufacturer.*

Mill Graded Irregular Customers: *Discount Retail Chains, Bargain Outlets, Warehouse Discount Stores, Screen Printers*

Source:
https://www.rgriley.com/CloseoutAndIrregularApparelDef
initionsAndQualityRankings.html

My Two Cents on Quality Levels

Garment Quality level is important to pay attention to when you are buying blank apparel to sell your clothing brand.

I recommend sticking with First Quality to be safe. This way, if your hoodie or t-shirt is a massive hit, you can go back and re-order more and know exactly the quality of the garment you will receive. Also, your cost will be usually fixed, meaning it won't fluctuate much for the most part.

If you want to get creative and score some deals, you can check out Closeouts.

Closeouts are first quality merchandise which, for some reason, has been taken "off the shelves" but is still in the first-quality condition.

Closeouts can be an option where you score great deals on merchandise, but just be cautious or aware of why it did not sell enough for the retailer and why it might have ended up in close-outs.

Also, remember you cannot reorder closeouts. Usually, this is the last run or something which the manufacturer will never produce again. If your customers love them, it will be hard for you to buy more at the same price point if the closeout vendor

Regardless, I have scored amazing deals with closeouts. One example of this is some Champion Sweaters, which we bought some time ago.

I was on RGRiley.com, one of our closeout suppliers, and saw these beautiful golden yellow Champion crewnecks. They were listed, I believe, for $4/pc. There was nothing wrong with them. They were just not selling as well as expected. This buying from first-quality wholesalers would have cost us $15+ per pc. We were able to buy these for $4/pc and take them to the screen printer to get them printed and sold them for $25+ per pc!

Sometimes you can get very lucky; sometimes you don't. Again this is luck sometimes and sometimes a fine dance between risk vs. reward.

Hand graded Irregulars usually have something wrong with them, but sometimes the defect might be a cut label. A cut label means that literally, the tag on the back of the shirt might be cut with scissors.

I would recommend you might want to avoid these usually just to be safe. However, if you plan to remove the tags anyway and get your own tags applied, you might just save some cost of your garments.

We will cover how to get your own tags later in the book.

So you do have some options when it comes to garment quality and suppliers, but, I would just recommend sticking to First Quality and maybe if you want to get creative, closeouts.

Sourcing Blank Apparel to Get Printed

If you think you want to get pre-made blanks as the blank apparel choice for your brand, there are a few ways to go about doing this.

⇨ Option #1: Have your decorator order your goods.

First, usually, the person who is screen printing or embroidering your garments can provide these for you. They will usually have a vendor account set up with wholesale apparel companies. These companies have these accounts set up and can usually order in the garments for you so that you don't have to worry about it.

The drawback for this is some, if not most, will usually have an upcharge on the garment itself.

For example, let's assume that the wholesaler charges them $2.00 per t-shirt. The screen printer or embroidery person will usually charge you $2.50 per t-shirt on top of any printing charges etc. which we will cover later in the book.

However, sometimes they do have discounts applied to their account due to their volume purchasing. This is something usually you want to call them to have a discussion to find out how they operate.

You can cross-check the price with what you can get them for vs. what they will be charging you for the blank.

⇨ **Option #2: Order your own goods.**

The next option which you have is to order your own goods separately. This basically means that you order the goods by yourself and ship them to your garment decorator. Sometimes, based on your relationships with suppliers and negotiating abilities, you can find a good deal.

Almost all suppliers will have a fixed price on all goods. The area of the type of goods which you might be able to score a good detail below the original garment

An example of suppliers which you might have

Neck Labels:

Usually, when you buy garments, they come with a little tag in the back neck area. This is called a tag/neck label etc. They come with the manufacturers' label, which includes washing instructions, size, and name of the brand.

It is actually possible for you to remove the manufacturers' labels and apply your own label.

I think this definitely steps up the professionalism of your brand; however, try to be cost-effective when you go about doing this. This can easily add $2 per piece to your final garment cost if you are producing in small quantities.

I would recommend not go this route unless you source a great deal on neck tag labels, or you are ordering some big quantities (300+).

Usually, you should find a screen printing/embroidery vendor who offers this finishing service. We offer this at our company merchn.com, but a lot of screen-printers and embroidery vendors do not offer this option as it involves a lot of work and is a niche request.

You have three options here.

Written By Yaswanth Nukasani ©
www.yaswanthnukasani.com

1. You can either get a "woven label" and sow it on to the garment or have your garment decorator sow it on for you. You can find companies which make garment care labels or "woven labels" on Google if you search "custom woven labels."

2. You can have your screenprinter do what is called a "neck label print," which basically instead of any sewing, they rip off the manufacturer's label and screenprint your tag on the back neck area of the garment.

3. You can get "heat-transfer labels," which allow you to basically heat-press your labels on with a heat press or an iron box.

"The Textile and Wool Acts require that labels contain three pieces of information pertaining to the garment: fiber content, country of origin, and

manufacturer, importer or dealer. The Care Labeling Rule requires that care instructions for the garment also be revealed."

- *Fiber content of the clothing;*
- *Country of origin;*
- *Manufacturer/dealer identity; and*
- *Care instructions*

https://www.intouch-quality.com/blog/how-to-comply-with-legal-requirements-for-clothing-labeling

Make sure to include all the required information on your label. To design your label, you can hire someone on Fiverr, or you can design it yourself on Adobe Illustrator, Photoshop, etc.

They also have "clothing label templates," which you can download from Google.

Blank Garments Suppliers List

There can be many suppliers, but these are some which I have worked with or would recommend over the years.

First Quality Wholesalers (Industry Standard)
- S&S Activewear: www.ssactivewear.com
- Alphabroder: www.alphabroder.com
- Carolina Made: www.carolinamade.com

- Apparel N' Bags: www.apparelnbags.com
- Jiffy Shirts: www.jiffyshirts.com

Closeout and/or Hand Graded Irregulars Wholesaler
- RG Riley: www.rgriley.com (I only included one because I have found these guys to be the best at what they do in the closeout, hand-grated irregular space)

* Remember each of these suppliers has their own strengths and weaknesses, please make sure to do your homework before making any decisions*

Written By Yaswanth Nukasani ©
www.yaswanthnukasani.com

CHAPTER: How to Get Designs Made

→ Getting a Logo Made
→ What to Tell and Give to Your Graphic Designer (Concept PDF)
→ Getting Merch Designs Made
→ Finding & Sourcing a Great Designer
→ Fiverr.com
→ Filtering Graphic Designers to Find a Good One
→ Hiring Designers
   ◆ Craigslist
   ◆ Behance
→ Does Your Partner do Graphic Design?

Written By Yaswanth Nukasani ©
www.yaswanthnukasani.com

Getting a Logo Made

There are probably better sources of information than me to talk about logo design, the psychology of colors, and design theory when it comes to getting a logo made.

In this part, I want to focus on the actual process of getting a logo made, such as communicating with a designer, finding a good designer, and some key pointers which I have found helpful over the years.

When getting a logo made, I have found it to be worthwhile to invest in a great designer. Depending on your financials, it can be hard to spend $100s or $1000s of dollars on hiring a fancy designer

I have found www.fiverr.com to be helpful in this process.

You can hire talented designers to design a logo for you starting from $5+. When starting a brand, I found that it takes a couple tries to get your

Next, I am going to cover how to pick and seperate great designers from the not-so-great designers.

This is where I have gone to most times to create logos and apparel designs for my brand.

Separating the Great vs. Not-So-Great Designers

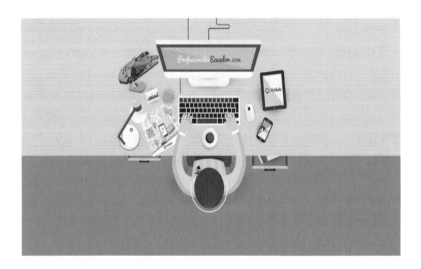

There are a LOT of graphic designers out there. However, not all do great work. Design is an important part of your brand, and it is something I would not compromise on.

To find great designers, it will come down to your ability to filter out talent.

There are a lot of Not-so-great designers out there, especially, on the

What Great Designers Do:
- Seem to have their own style of art, which they produce, which seems consistent in their portfolio.
- Usually, create it from scratch. They usually draw it by hand and then turn it into a digital art on the computer.
- Most times use very little, if not none, stock clipart, etc. if your designs
- Understand colors, shading, style.
- Seem to be more interested in creating your art than the focus on getting paid.
- Have a lot of repeat customers

What Not-So-Great Designers Do:
- Use Un-original artwork & use stock clip-art from various website and slap your name on it and call it a design.
- Usually, don't create vector art in professional graphic designer software such as Adobe Photoshop, Adobe Illustrator.

- Aren't educated in design/art fundamentals.
- Don't usually have past work/portfolio examples. (Even if they are new to the game, they can, of course, just create sample artwork. This, to me, shows a lack of initiative.)
- Overly focused on the compensation $$ part
- Lack of confidence in their work and undervalue their work.

Here are 7 designers which most I have worked with in the past, which I believe do great work:

Almost all of them have been through Fiverr.com

1. Great for Logos - Fiverr: vicklevko
2. Great for Designs - Fiverr: olegkravets
3. issacristina
4. aminebenaiss
5. magyarmelcsi
6. littlepinecone
7. steffengrafisk

Getting Designs Made for Your Apparel a.k.a "Merch"

Once you have found a great designer who fits your price range and you have a logo, let us start creating cool designs for your merchandise. (t-shirts, hats, hoodies, etc.)

To get a merch design made, FIRST, make sure to read the second half of this book to understand printing methods. Your designs will turn out better if you tailor your designs to the nature of the printing method you choose.

Simply put, some designs work well with screenprinting, and some work better with embroidery.

For example, embroidery involves thread and stitching. Embroidery does not work with certain types of art. For example, if you are trying to embroider a digital photographic picture, that will be a disaster.

Embroidery works better with simpler/cleaner art.

I will go into more detail in the second half of the book about printing methods and how they work. Make sure to read that!

What to Tell and Give to Your Graphic Designer (Concept PDF): I would recommend creating a small document on Word and sending them a PDF of your instructions, which they should follow in bringing your vision to life.

Example of one of our old concept documents below:

Graphic Tee - Design Concept

"SENECA" ADULT T-SHIRT

Main Text: "DE BREVITATE VITA"

Garment Colors: Black #000000 & White (#ffffff)

Garment: ON BLACK OR ROYAL T-SHIRT FRONT

Style: Streetwear   Rock   Vintage   Tee
Add Text: Subtext: They loose the day in expectation of the night and the night in fear of the dawn.

Add Vertical Text (very small): SENCA THE YOUNGER X THE PHI CONCEPT 49 A.D.

Use multiple colors which you believe is appropriate. Maximum 4 colors. As little color as necessary.

Use this drawing of Seneca (MAIN OBJECT #1)

REMOVE BACKGROUND   + MAIN OBJECT #2 – HOURGLASS

Meaning: Life will follow the path it began to take, and will neither reverse nor check its course. It will cause no commotion to remind you of its swiftness, but glide on quietly. It will not lengthen itself for a king's command or a people's favor. As it started on its first day, so it will run on, nowhere pausing or turning aside. What will be the outcome? You have been preoccupied while life hastens on. Meanwhile, death will arrive, and you have no choice in making yourself available for that."

Example of style:

Vintage Rock Retro Streetwear T-Shirts

DESIGN WILL BE PLACED ON

FRONT BIG

Other Ways to Hire Great Designers (Craigslist, Social Media, Behance)

There are plenty of other ways to source great design talent. The ones which I have listed in the book are what have worked well for me and found these to work well.

Behance:
Behance is a social media platform owned by Adobe which aims "to showcase and discover creative work."

- Action Step: Find great designers that you love and then send them a Direct Message on Instagram or Email them saying you saw them on Behance and want to work with them for your clothing brand, ask for their portfolio & pricing.

Social Media:
Twitter, Instagram, Facebook!
- Action Step:
    1. Make a post on your social that you are looking for a graphic designer to work with for your brand.
    2. Search by hashtags for "artists," etc.
    3. Find graphic designer art shoutout accounts and slide into the DMs!

Dribbble:
Dribbble is a self-promotion and social networking platform for digital designers and creatives. It serves as

a design portfolio platform, jobs, and recruiting site and is one of the largest platforms for designers to share their work online.

- <u>Action Step:</u> Find great designers that you love and then send them a Direct Message on Instagram or Email them saying you saw them on Behance and want to work with them for your clothing brand, ask for their portfolio & pricing.

Craigslist: *Craigslist is an American classified advertisements website with sections devoted to jobs, housing, for sale, items wanted, services, community service, gigs, résumés, and discussion forums.*

<u>Does Your Partner do Graphic Design?</u>

One final source is you, or if you have a partner, can learn how to do graphic design. This can be an option if you have some time on your hands!

You can even charge others to do graphic design and make that a side hustle to put more money into your brand :)

CHAPTER: Decoration Method #1: Screenprinting

- → How Screenprinting Works
  - ◆ The Pros of Screenprinting
  - ◆ The Cons of Screenprinting
  - ◆ Why You Probably Shouldn't DIY Screenprint
- → Getting Your First Merch Drop Screenprinted
  - ◆ Art
    - ● Art: Getting Art Made
    - ● Art: Vector vs. Raster
  - ◆ Ink Colors
  - ◆ Sizing & Quantity
  - ◆ Blank Garment
    - ●
  - ◆ Locations
- → Sizing
- → Ink Colors
- → Ink Types
  - ◆ Plastisol Ink
  - ◆ Traditional
  - ◆ Puff
  - ◆ Soft Hand
  - ◆ Waterbased Ink
  - ◆ Discharge Ink
- → Underbases and Dark Garments
- → Different Garment Types & Fabrics
- → Locations
- → Traditional Locations vs. Speciality Locations

→ Print Options
- ◆ Spot Color
- ◆ 4-Color
- ◆ Simulated Process
- ◆ Additional Services to Ask About

→ Understanding Pricing
- ◆ Focus to Save on Garment Cost
- ◆ Different Type of Printers
- ◆ How to Get the Best Pricing on Screenprinting Services

Overview of Screen Printing

Screen printing is probably one of the most popular printing or "decorating" method when it comes to apparel. Most graphic tees etc. are printed through this method. A lot of the "Nike Just Do It" T-Shirts are printed like this. Hoodies, t-shirts, crewnecks, etc. are mostly always screen printed with various designs for various purposes. (collegiate wear, fashion t-shirts, marathon/running tees, beach/vacation tees)

What is Screen Printing?

Screen Printing - Technically Speaking

One screen (mesh stencil) is used for each color to be printed - screens must be lined up (or registered) and printed on test sheets to ensure that all of the colors line up correctly. Inks are then pushed through the screens one color at a time onto the apparel. Finally, each piece is run through a large dryer to cure the inks.

How Does screenprinting Work?

Ink + screen (mesh stencil) = screenprinting! Luckily, the screen printing process itself has very little limits on what surfaces can be used to print on. Staying on trend is easy-peasy with this process, considering all of the awesome ink types available that can manipulate the "look" of the final print. Expert printers understand the relationships between the various inks, shirt materials, and shirt colors - with this knowledge, and we're able to help achieve the look you're going for.

https://www.threadbird.com/the-screen-printing-process

What Type of Garments are Usually Screen Printed?

For your brand, here are some types of garments that you can get screen printed.

- T-Shirts
- Hoodies

- Long Sleeve Tees
- V-Neck Tees
- Racerback Tank Tops
- Sweatpants
- Crewnecks

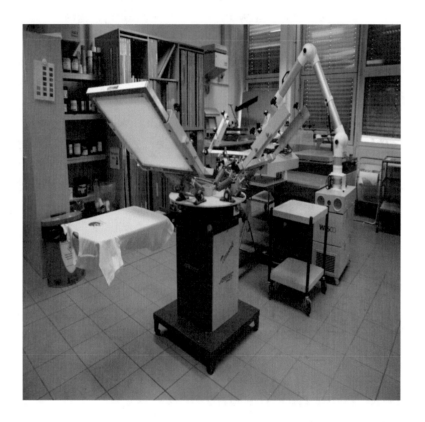

The Pros of Screenprinting

- Lowered printing cost as your buy more bulk quantities
- High accurate digital replication of artwork (meaning that the artwork which you design on

the computer can look very close or similar when it is actually printed onto the garment)
- You can print big designs without too much extra cost. (with embroidery you printing cost changes by how many stitches is in the artwork, usually the bigger the artwork in embroidery, the more expensive it is.)
- Simple and silhouette-based designs end up saving cost on printing

The Cons of Screen Printing
- Higher Minimum Order Quantity on prints. (Usually, you have to order 24 pieces at the minimum, to get good pricing you have to order 50+ pieces at least and to get great pricing, you have to order at least 144-300+ pieces to be printed)
- More colorful artwork tends to be more expensive to print.
- Each color you have to pay for what is called a "screen setup charge." Basically, it takes the screen-printer time and money to create each additional screen.

Why You Probably Shouldn't "DIY" Screenprint

If you are thinking about screen printing your own t-shirts and not outsourcing it to a manufacturer, be sure to read about why I think you should not try to do it yourself.

Written By Yaswanth Nukasani ©
www.yaswanthnukasani.com

Screen Printing is a process that, on the surface, seems very easy and straightforward. It is. However, I have tried screen printing in the past, and it turned out to be a total nightmare from a quality standpoint.

The reason I tried to screen print my own goods in the past is to avoid paying the decoration cost to other screen printers and keep our costs down. The reality of the situation was screen printing equipment, and supplies can be expensive if you simply don't have a high volume output or scale when it comes to printing. You also need space to store it.

Also, there can be a lot of errors made in printing, which will affect the quality or output of your final product. When we started, we messed up 100s of t-shirts on prints because our equipment was not good, and we also lacked professional screen printing experience.

Now, through my printing company Merchn.com, we outsource all of our printing to professional screen printers and still end up paying less than what it would cost us to print it ourselves. Many clothing brands who used to try to print themselves switched over to our company and ended up saving tons of money, time, and improved the quality of their product at the end.

For your clothing brand, most of the value generation will come down to your ability to do marketing. Any time spent on production, I feel distracts you from spending time on your business.

Few reasons may be you could consider printing yourself:

1. You already have a professional screen printing experience.
2. You inherited or own screen printing presses and equipment already.
3. You love the art of screenprinting and actually enjoying doing the manual printing yourself.

Your total upfront cost to start printing yourself will also be a couple of thousand dollars just for the equipment alone.

I have found it to work far better for us to outsource to industry professionals.

If you need help with this, feel free to get in touch with me. Our printing company already prints for many other clothing brands for half the price of what it would cost you elsewhere.

Getting Your First Batch of Merch Screen Printed

So now you are ready to start getting your first batch of t-shirts or whatever other merchandise printed. There are five main things that you need to understand when it comes to getting your first batch screen printed.

Written By Yaswanth Nukasani ©
www.yaswanthnukasani.com

 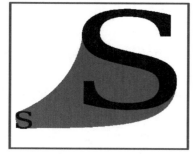

Raster
.jpeg .gif .png

Vector
.svg

Art:

Now that you know how to find a graphic designer and get art made, for screenprinting, you need to get a type of art file called "Vector File" or "Vector Art." You don't even need to understand, all you need to tell your designer is "I need an adobe illustrator vector file for this artwork design."

The technical and fancy definition is as follows:

Raster artwork is any digital art composed of horizontal and vertical rows of pixels. ... Vector artwork is digital art composed of mathematical lines and curves. As a result, vector images can be reduced or enlarged in size indefinitely, without any loss in image quality.
Source:
https://www.customink.com/help_center/raster-vs-vector-art

For Example:

Sometimes when you save an image on your phone, when you zoom out, it looks fine! However, when you zoom in on it, it starts to become blurry. This is raster art.

Vector art allows you to zoom in on it, make it bigger or smaller without losing the details in the artwork. There is no loss of quality from making objects bigger, smaller, or zooming in on them.
So again, You don't even need to understand this; all you need to do is tell your designer is "*I need an adobe illustrator vector file for this artwork design.*"

If they can't make a vector file for you, you can just go on Fiverr.com as mentioned earlier and search for "vector art" and hire someone to do it for you for $5.

Ink Colors:

When you print things from a normal inkjet printer for documents, photos, etc. in a color you utilize this process called "CMYK" usually. It stands for Cyan, Magenta, Yellow & Black. Basically, when you print something from an inkjet printer, your image or colors in your prints are produced from a mixture of these 4 colors.

When you get screen printed t-shirts, you usually utilize a more accurate type of color called "Spot Color" most of the time.

In Spot Color, you use ink, which is exactly that color. If your printer used spot colors, there would be a gazillion different cartridges. In screen printing, to produce accurate color and not a mixed color effect, the industry most commonly uses spot color.

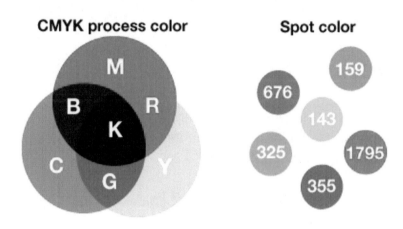

Remember, screen printing actually involves real ink. The most common one is "plastisol ink." We will talk about the other ink types later.

The two things you actually need to remember out of all this color stuff is *PANTONE MATCH* vs. *STOCK COLOR*.

STOCK COLOR

Stock Color is quite simple. This is usually the selection of ink colors, which screen printers will keep on hand as they will use them quite often.

Most of them will have a "stock color ink chart," which shows you which colors they have in-house for you to use. They cannot keep every ink color in inventory because it can become costly to store 100s of colors as a gallon of plastisol ink is around $50+ etc.

Often if your colors are quite simple and do not have pastel or other fancy colors involved, you can ask them to "match your artwork as close to the inks they have available.

However, if your artwork does have complex colors (pastel, comfort colors, etc.), you can ask about Pantone matching.

PANTONE MATCH COLOR

There are apparently 18 decillion colors that exist. Most of these are shades of different main colors.

Few examples of Main Colors: blue, yellow, red (Shades of Blue, yellow, red)

Pantone is the industry leader in the color space. Most printers use this color system called the "Pantone Matching System." This basically helps you communicate the exact shade of color you want to be translated in your print.

Pantone colors are color codes that stand for a specific shade. You can communicate about colors by defining the Pantone code. Basically, the Pantone is the standard language for colors.

The formula developed by Pantone is a spot color. This means that the color is created from a palette of 18 basic colors, not with screens or dots.

Process colors are CMYK colors; the color is determined by cyan, magenta, yellow, and black. There are more Pantone colors because not all colors can be mixed in CMYK.

https://blog.merchandise-essentials.com/what-are-pantone-colors

Once you provide a Pantone Code to your screen printer, most of them will be able to mix the exact shade of color which you are looking for.

They usually charge $35+ per color, depending on the company. So, if possible and if it's not crucial, stick to stock color.

You can go on www.pantone.com, and you will be able to explore colors and find more information.

Sizing & Quantity

When you think about T-Shirt or Apparel Sizes, these are usually the most common choices. Before you place your first order, it is often helpful to think of how many of each you would like to have.

- Extra Small
- Small
- Medium
- Large
- Extra Large
- 2XL
- 3XL
- 4XL
- 5XL
- And so, on.

Blank Garment

As you slowly put together all the details of your order to get merch made, another thing to keep in mind is your Blank Garment choice.

There are many blank garment brands in the U.S.

The most common ones with the best reliability and availability, in my opinion, are below...

Brands:
- Standard
  - Gildan
  - Hanes
- Premium (Recommended)
  - Bella + Canvas
  - American Apparel
  - Next Level
  - Champion
  - Independent Trading Co.
  - Alternative Apparel

Our company offers all these and 100s of other brands at wholesale prices to you, so if you would like, get in touch with me, and we can get your brand manufactured.!

There are many other brands available to see more options, head to *https://www.ssactivewear.com/brands*

Locations

Design-wise, and you need to pick where your design placements are going to be. This means where on the garment would you like your design/logo to be placed.

In screen printing, you are charged for every location where you place your design. So the more locations, the more cost. However, it's marginally more expensive, and you can look at a quote break down for more details. It is up to you to decide if it's crucial to have lots of locations for your design.

Some specialty locations have an up-charge if they are hard to print; it depends on the screenprinter...

Below I have included a chart for you to be aware of the imprint locations available to you:

IMPRINT SIZING CHART (SCREENPRINTING)

The following chart provides suggested artwork imprint sizes for screenprinting projects.

- Each box represents a different set-up even if the art is the same.
- Custom placements are available.
- We do not offer "all over" printing.
- Pullover hoods have height limitations due to the front pocket.
- Gildan G2000B youth shirts can accommodate prints up to 13" wide.
- Embroidery is recommended for baseball caps but 1 color prints can be done.
- Embroidery is recommended for lined jackets but in some cases multi color printing can be done.

FULL FRONT
Suggested Imprint Size:
Adult:8.0" to 13.0" Wide
Youth:6.0" to 9.5" Wide
Infant:3.0" to 5.5" Wide
Suggested Imprint Size:
Adult:15.0" Wide to 15.0" High
Youth:9.5" Wide
Infant:5.5" Wide

ON THE POCKET
Suggested Imprint Size:
3.0" Wide

Maximum Imprint Size:
3.5" Wide

RIGHT/LEFT HIP
Suggested Imprint Size:
3.0" to 4.0" Wide

Maximum Imprint Size:
5.5" Wide

SMALL FRONT
Suggested Imprint Size:
5" to 7.0" Wide

Maximum Imprint Size:
15.0" Wide

FULL BACK
Suggested Imprint Size:
8.0" to 13.0" Wide

Maximum Imprint Size:
15.0" Wide x 15.0" High

RIGHT/LEFT LONG LEG
Suggested Imprint Size:
3.0" to 4.0" Wide
10.0 "to 14.0" Long

Maximum Imprint Size:
5.5" Wide x 15.0" Long

LEFT CHEST
Suggested Imprint Size:
2.5" to 4.0" Wide

Maximum Imprint Size:
4.0" Wide x 4.0" High

LOCKER PATCH
Suggested Imprint Size:
1" to 4" Wide

RIGHT/LEFT OVERSIZED LEG
Suggested Imprint Size:
3.0" to 4.0" Wide
22.0" Long

Maximum Imprint Size:
5.5" Wide x 22.0" Long

RIGHT CHEST
Suggested Imprint Size:
2.5" to 4.0" Wide

Maximum Imprint Size:
4.0" Wide x 4.0" High

RIGHT/LEFT SHOULDER SHORT/LONG SLEEVE
Suggested Imprint Size:
2.0" to 4.0" Wide

Maximum Imprint Size:
5.5" Wide

RIGHT/LEFT SHORTS
Suggested Imprint Size:
3.0" to 4.0" Wide

Maximum Imprint Size:
5.5" Wide

ABOVE POCKET
Suggested Imprint Size:
2.5" to 4.0" Wide

Maximum Imprint Size:
4.0" Wide x 3.0" High

RIGHT/LEFT LONG SLEEVE
Suggested Imprint Size:
2.0" to 3.0" Wide
10.0" to 12.0" Long

Maximum Imprint Size:
3.5" Wide x 15.0" Long

Image provided by St. Croix Print

Ink Types:

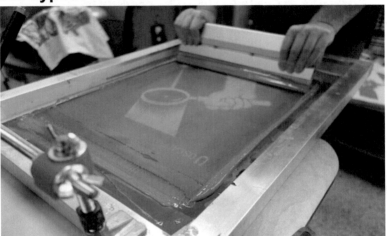

In screen printing, for the most part, traditional plastisol ink is used. However, sometimes there are specialty inks available that produce different types of effects and feel on the garment.

→ <u>Traditional Plastisol Ink</u>: Most people involved in screen printing tend to use Plastisol ink. It is thick, durable, versatile, and provides clear graphic detail. Plastisol ink is also easy to mix, long-lasting, widely available, comes in a wide array of colors, and works well with a wide range of screen printing methods, equipment, and designs. It can also stay on the screen for long periods of time without drying out. This type of ink's high density prevents it from arching, and its low viscosity allows it to work well with softer prints. It also provides a low gloss, flat finish. Plastisol ink needs heat to dry.

→ Water-Based Ink: Some people prefer water-based ink because it soaks into the fibers of the fabric on which it is used rather than sitting on top of it as Plastisol does. This gives the screen print a softer feel compared to those made using Plastisol ink. Some people find it provides the print with a more solid feel as well. Plus, water-based inks are easy to use, even for printers without much experience or skill. However, it can take a longer time to dry in humid conditions and may require the use of a heat source. This type of ink is semi-transparent and may require custom color matching to produce a uniform look throughout the garment. It may also need a high count mesh screen and a retarder to prevent flooding of the design.

→ Discharge Ink: Discharge ink is available in both Plastisol and water-based types. When using discharge ink, the ink removes the color of the fabric on the areas where it is applied and replaces it with its pigment. This makes discharge ink a popular choice for people working with 100% cotton. It is necessary to use a heat source in order for fabrics silkscreened with discharge ink to cure fully. Using this type of ink does require a fairly high level of expertise.

The type of ink that you should choose to do your screen printing depends on a number of factors. These include the type of application, space restrictions, environmental concerns, economic limitations, and end goals. Water-based ink has risen in popularity due to its eco-friendly reputation. New Plastisol inks are being developed to be environmentally safe as well.

Source: https://welogoit.com/blog/2018/05/types-of-ink-used-in-screen-printing

Underbases and Dark Garments

Since when screen-printing your laying down a thin layer wet ink on the fabric, if the garment color is dark, most times, the garment color will bleed through the ink. This means if you are using a black t-shirt and printing yellow on it, there will be little black dots through the yellow ink.

Sometimes, this can be used to create a vintage look or faded look.
However, if you are going for a crisp detailed print, you will want to use what is called an under base.

Your screenprinter will mention this to you, but it is good to understand this.

An underbase is a layer of white ink that is laid down on the garment, and then the remainder of the colors will be printed on top of this layer.

Since you are printing on top of the white layer of ink (under base), your images will come out more detailed and sharp.

An under base will add to your print cost, like adding another color to your print. It will usually cost you a bit more than just printing on a white or light-colored garment.

We will cover the pricing structure next.

Understanding Pricing

1st Print Location

Quantity	1 Color	2 Colors	3 Colors	4 Colors	5 Colors	6 Colors	7 Colors	8+ Colors
25+	8.00	10.00	12.00	14.00	16.00			
50+	7.00	8.50	10.00	11.50	13.00	14.50		
100+	6.50	7.50	8.50	9.50	10.50	11.50	12.50	Custom
250+	6.00	6.75	7.50	8.25	9.00	9.75	10.50	Custom
500+	5.50	6.00	6.50	7.00	7.50	8.00	8.50	Custom
1000+	5.00	5.50	6.00	6.50	7.00	7.50	8.00	Custom
2500+	Custom	Custom	Custom	Custom	Custom	Custom	Custom	Custom

2nd Print Location

Quantity	1 Color	2 Colors	3 Colors	4 Colors	5 Colors	6 Colors	7 Colors	8+ Colors
25+	+3.00	+4.50	+6.00	+7.50	+9.00			
50+	+2.00	+3.00	+4.00	+5.00	+6.00	+7.00		
100+	+1.50	+2.25	+3.00	+3.75	+4.50	+5.25	+6.00	Custom
250+	+1.00	+1.50	+2.00	+2.50	+3.00	+3.50	+4.00	Custom
500+	+0.75	+1.25	+1.75	+2.25	+2.75	+3.25	+3.75	Custom
1000+	+0.50	+0.85	+1.15	+1.50	+1.85	+2.20	+2.55	Custom
2500+	Custom	Custom	Custom	Custom	Custom	Custom	Custom	Custom

Written By Yaswanth Nukasani ©
www.yaswanthnukasani.com

If you just send your artwork to your screen printer and tell them what type of garment you want to use and the details, they will get back to you with a quote. You do not need to know how the pricing structure works, but it is often helpful to understand what affects the price and quote you receive.

On a basic level, the variables which will affect your screenprinting prices are:

- # of colors in your design (this will increase your per piece print cost, and it will also increase your setup cost per screen) *(More color, more $$)*
- # of locations (ex: front, back, etc.) *(More locations, more $$)*
- Your order quantity (how many pieces you are getting printed, the more you print, the cheaper) (More quantity, LESS $$)
- Any other special requests you might have (Pantone match colors, special inks, packaging, labeling, etc.)

The more colors you order, the more work and time it is for your screen-printer. So, to set up each print, if there are 5 colors in your design, it will take 5 screens to print each individual color. Usually, they will charge a flat setup fee of around $20 per screen.

Formula: 1st Location = (Setup Cost for screen * # of screens) + (# of pcs being printed * print cost per pc)

Repeat for the second location and so on...

For example:

Let's say you are getting a 1 location print with 2 colors...
Screen setup: $20
Quantity: 50

*($20 * 2 = $40) + (50 * $8.5/pc) = $465*

$465 / 50 pcs = $9.3 per piece

So it would cost you $9.30 per piece for each shirt to get printed. Don't forget to add your garment cost.

How to Get the Best Pricing on Screen Printing Services

- Focus also on saving on Garment Cost.

This isn't technically how to get the best pricing on screen printing services, but also keep in mind that along with your print cost, your garment cost is also something which is a significant percentage of your production cost when it comes to the overall cost of your product. I would recommend you go on Amazon or somewhere and order a few samples at a few different price points or even ask your screen-printer to send samples of a couple of different choices of shirts you are thinking about.

- Reduce the colors in your designs.

  The next option you have in reducing your print cost is to chill out with the colors! Meaning, don't use too many! Though we might assume more color could mean the design looks better or something of that sort. Not always! If you look at the best selling screen printed streetwear graphic tees, they always seem to focus on using the silhouette, shapes more than 13 different colors.

- Reduce the number of locations.

  Unless the style of your brand or the integrity of the design needs or must have printed all over the garment, I would say to keep it minimal. I often side with just front or front and back. Unless I am going to produce a high volume of apparel, then I might add sleeves, etc.

- Increase the quantity of your order.
  If your first initial run went well and you think you have the traction and budget to invest in high volume runs, go for it! You start seeing massive savings at around 300+ order quantity.

- Negotiate & Get more quotes!

Different Type of Printers

Due to the nature of the screen printing manufacturing process, many companies have to pick a business model. Often they can focus on higher-margin orders and

- The retail printers:
    - High margin, low volume.
        - For example, $2 profit per pc * 100 (#of pcs printed) = $200
- The contract/wholesale printers:
    - Lower margin, higher volume.
        - For example, $1 profit per pc * 300 (#of pcs printed) = $300

I always work with larger wholesale/contract screen printers. The main reason for this, their business is set up in a way that allows them to charge you less per piece as their focus is to print a higher volume of pieces every month.

To work with contract/wholesale printers, time and efficiency is of the essence for them. You will need to have your stuff together.

- Quantity & Size Breakdowns
- Vector Artwork
- Garment Color Choice & Model #
- Shipping Address
- In-Bound Goods Delivery Details (if your shipping, when will your goods arrive to the printers)
- Placements (know where you want to place your designs/logo on the garment)
- Deadline (if you have a date which you absolutely must need this by, communicate this with them)

Usually, sending one email with all the required info and artwork is the best practice. Some of them will make you fill out an order form, which will also have similar information to the one listed above.

If you go to merchn.com/brand and mention you got this book when you call us, I will hop on the phone with you and give you great wholesale pricing personally to help you launch your brand. We are a wholesale/contract apparel manufacturing company.

Feel free to also reach out on Instagram @yaswanthnukasani as well with any questions you might have.

Print Options

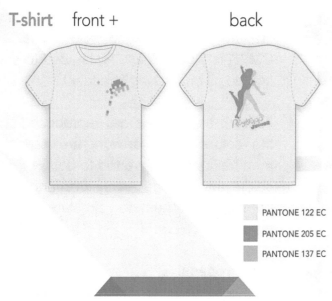

PANTONE 122 EC
PANTONE 205 EC
PANTONE 137 EC

→ **Spot Color:**
- ◆ Spot colors are printed with premixed inks on a printing press or screen-printer. Each spot color is reproduced using a single printing plate or screen. To ensure that a printer uses the exact color that the designer intends, the Pantone Matching System (PMS) is used.

→ **4-Color / CMYK:**

- ◆ Process color printing, also known as four-color process printing, is a method that reproduces finished full-color artwork and photographs. The three primary colors used are cyan (process blue), magenta (process red), and yellow. These inks are translucent and are used to simulate different colors; for example, green can be created using cyan and yellow. The "K" in CMYK is black. Black ink is used to create fine detail and strong shadows.

- ◆ Artwork and photos are reproduced when the colors in the artwork are separated, then halftoned (converted to dots). Process colors are reproduced by overlapping and printing halftones to simulate a large number of colors.

→ **Simulated Process:**

- ◆ This process is similar to 4-Color / CMYK, except the simulated process is used for dark garments.

https://www.mam-a.com/process_spot_printing

MAJOR HACK: How I Printed My Own Shirts when I started and How you can to...

Screen Printing charges can rack up very quickly and might limit how many items and designs you produce.

I want to share one hack which I have used in the past, which has solved this problem for me. This hack involves you having to do the work and the printing yourself but can help you save decoration costs. You can print using this method for 15 cents per print!

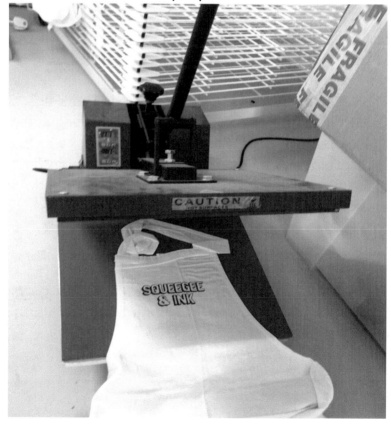

Things You Need:

- 15 x 15-inch Heat Press (any heat press big enough works but this is the minimum size I recommend for printing shirts) - $160
- Screen Printed Plastisol Transfers - as low as 15 cents per piece.

This would be a one-time investment for the heat press, but it is a machine which you can press as many apparel pieces

Method:

1. Buy a Heat Press
2. Order "Plastisol Screen Printed Transfers" on fmexpressions.com (I recommend looking at their one color, two-color, and full-color
3. Turn on the heat press. Apply for the transfer by placing it where you want your design/logo to be and pulling down the handle of the heat press.

More detailed instructions are below.

There are many YouTube videos on this. Just google "plastisol transfers" on youtube, and there are tutorials on how to print each shirt.

Written By Yaswanth Nukasani ©
www.yaswanthnukasani.com

Here is an example of one of F&M's program:

ONE COLOR PROGRAM

AVAILABLE IN: VINTAGE | ATHLETIC | PERFORMANCE | NYLON

Simply the best deal on one color heat transfer in the industry. As low as 15¢ per piece for our Athletic or Nylon formulas (plus setup) for any single image up to 9" by 12.75". Or, get our premium Vintage formula for as low as 45¢ per piece plus setup. The setup fee applies to each order.

How To Apply for Our Transfers

Applying our transfers is super simple. Follow the steps and instructions below to achieve perfect results on your next project!

1) No Teflon Sheets, Covers, or Pillows. Ever.

Never use teflon sheets, covers, or pillows with any of our plastisol formulas. They dissipate the heat too much, resulting in a poorly applied transfer.

2) Calibrate Your Heat Press.

You will need to use a quality Infrared (IR) Temperature Gun (Contactless) to ensure your heat press is heating evenly and accurately. You should do this each and every time you start a new pressing cycle.

3) Pressure, Pressure, Pressure.

Plastisol transfers will give you a quality and long-lasting decoration solution, but you HAVE to ensure you are using adequate and even pressure. This will ensure the formula properly adheres to your garment. Not using enough pressure can result in poorly applied plastisol transfers.

4) Water-resistant, waterproof, and fireproof garments:

We recommend testing a sample on your item before production. Water-resistant, waterproof, and fireproof garments may not accept a heat transfer application.

Athletic Formula

NO TEFLON SHEETS, COVERS or PILLOWS
Temperature: 325 Degrees Fahrenheit
Time: 7 Seconds

Pressure: High Pressure (8-9 Manual, 60PSI Automatic)
Peel: Hot Peel

Performance Formula

NO TEFLON SHEETS, COVERS or PILLOWS
Temperature: 300 Degrees Fahrenheit
Time: 7 Seconds
Pressure: Max Pressure (8-9 Manual, 60PSI Automatic)
Peel: Hot Peel

Fashion Formula (Lights, Darks, Spot)

NO TEFLON SHEETS, COVERS or PILLOWS
Temperature: 350 Degrees Fahrenheit
Time: 7 Seconds
Pressure: Max Pressure (8-9 Manual, 60PSI Automatic)
Peel: Hot Peel

Vintage Formula

NO TEFLON SHEETS, COVERS or PILLOWS
Temperature: 375 Degrees Fahrenheit
Time: 7 Seconds
Pressure: Max Pressure (8-9 Manual, 60PSI Automatic)
Peel: Hot Peel

Nylon Formula

NO TEFLON SHEETS, COVERS or PILLOWS

Temperature: 300 Degrees Fahrenheit
Time: 7 Seconds
Pressure: Max Pressure (8-9 Manual, 60PSI Automatic)
Peel: Hot Peel

Non-Woven Formula

NO TEFLON SHEETS, COVERS or PILLOWS
Temperature: 250 Degrees Fahrenheit
Time: 7 Seconds
Pressure: Max Pressure (8-9 Manual, 60PSI Automatic)
Peel: Hot Peel

Sublimation

NO TEFLON SHEETS, COVERS or PILLOWS
Temperature: 400 Degrees Fahrenheit
Time: 30 Seconds
Pressure: Medium Pressure (6-8 Manual, 50PSI Automatic)
Peel: Hot Peel

Foil Formula

NO TEFLON SHEETS, COVERS or PILLOWS
STEP 1 (Applying Foil Formula To Garment)

Temperature: 350 Degrees Fahrenheit
Time: 7 Seconds
Pressure: Max Pressure (8-9 Manual, 60PSI Automatic)

Peel: Hot Peel

STEP 2 (Applying Foil To Foil Formula)
Temperature: 350 Degrees Fahrenheit
Time: 7 Seconds
Pressure: Max Pressure (8-9 Manual, 60PSI Automatic)
Peel: Cold Peel

Waterbased Formula

NO TEFLON SHEETS, COVERS or PILLOWS
Temperature: 240-280 Degrees Fahrenheit
Time: 7 Seconds
Pressure: Max Pressure (8-9 Manual, 60PSI Automatic)
Peel: Hot Peel

https://support.fmexpressions.com/how-to-apply-our-transfers

CHAPTER: Decoration Methods (Embroidery)

Decoration Method #1: Embroidery

What is Embroidery?

Embroidery is the craft of decorating fabric or other materials using a needle to apply thread or yarn. Embroidery may also incorporate other materials such as pearls, beads, quills, and sequins.

A great example of embroidery is the notorious Ralph Lauren logo, Nautica logo, etc.

The Pros of Embroidery
- Low minimum
- # of colors in your design does not increase the cost.

The Cons of Embroidery
- Large designs can be expensive
- Larger designs can have a heavy feel on lighter garments

- Loss of fine details

Why You Probably Shouldn't DIY Embroidery

Just like screenprinting, embroidery also requires proper equipment and is also a skill. If you plan to embroider yourself, you will need to spend 1000s of dollars on equipment and supplies. A decent embroidery machine can start at $10,000+

For these reasons and some more, I think its best if you outsource your embroidery and focus on marketing your brand.

Getting Your First Merch Drop Embroidered Art

When thinking about designing designs or art for your embroidered design, there are a few things to keep in mind...

For embroidery, it is very hard to create "digital prints." Digital prints are the ones with a lot of details, shading, gradients, etc. For example, a photograph. In embroidery, you're using thread to decorate the garment and bring your design to life.

Working with threads can be tricky if you plan on having very complex artwork. Just think about it if you are trying to stitch out the artwork by hand, would this be even remotely possible?

A great "rule of thumb" for this is to make sure the artwork you or your graphic designer create is "vector artwork." This ensures that your art will be of high quality to create a crispy digitized embroidery file.

A couple of art types that work well are simple graphics. An example of this can be text/typography logos, simple cartoon art, vector line art, etc.

The type of art which won't work are photographs,

Digitization

Digitization, simply put, or at least how I think about it is taking your artwork and converting it to a file which the embroidery machine can read. (In the embroidery machine's "language")

Here is a more detail explanation which I found which might be useful for you to understand this:

In general, an embroidery art department can accept any type of artwork you provide right down to a sketch on a napkin. The important thing to remember is this: the better the art, the better the embroidery. The process for converting artwork to embroidery is called digitizing, and the artists that do it are called - you guessed it - digitizers. Basically, digitizing is redrawing a logo or design

Written By Yaswanth Nukasani ©
www.yaswanthnukasani.com

as stitches in a special embroidery software program designed to do just that.

Cleaner, more exact digital files allow the digitizer to be more exact with the stitch placement.
The stitch instructions are saved to a disk by a digitizer. An operator takes the disk and inserts it into the embroidery machine, which reads the instructions.

The ideal file formats are either Adobe Illustrator files (ai, eps, pdf) or high-resolution Adobe Photoshop files (psd, eps, tiff, jpg). Chances are, your digitizer can work with any other file type, Microsoft Word, for example, but there will likely be art fees incurred in order to redraw or re-create the image so the image can be cleanly digitized.

If your artwork involves lettering, you'll want to be sure the smallest letter is at least 1/4" tall. Smaller lettering will look messy or squashed. Superfine detail often does not translate well to embroidery. This can really only be assessed on a case by case basis. Should you have any questions about how well your logo or design will sew, just ask your decorator. Embroidery experts can help you make adjustments to maintain the integrity of your image or logo while improving the quality of the embroidery.
https://www.sharprint.com/blog/what-you-need-to-know-about-art-for-embroidery

Backing Paper

Along with thread, there is another part. The thread which is being punched into your garment needs something to latch on to. In embroidery, it latches onto something called "backing paper" or "stabilizer." I found this useful excerpt, which goes into detail into explaining the options which you have...

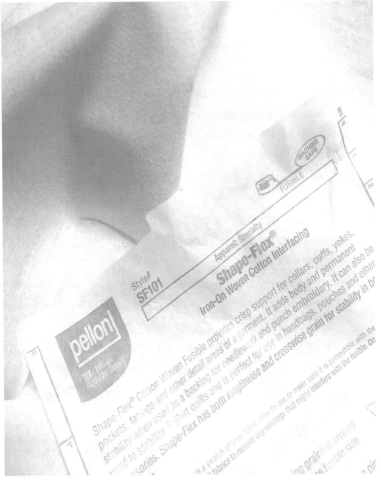

I recommend tear-away or water-soluble as it is discrete and goes away after washing...

What is the one thing that is almost never seen to anyone but the sewer, yet remains the most critical component of embroidery? Stabilizer! (or backing). The three basic types of stabilizer are tear-away, cutaway, and water-soluble. Choosing the right stabilizer for your project can be a tricky concept to master. Garment fabric, stitch density, color, stitch length, stitch speed, size of the embroidery, and stability of the design are just a few of the many variables to consider. The wrong backing can leave you with loose, inconsistent stitching that makes your work look poorly done.

Tear-Away

This type of stabilizer tears like paper. It can be thin and wispy, or it can be thick and crisp. This is a good overall backing that can be used for most projects. There are three main things to consider when using tear-away backing. One, make sure that you are using a quality stabilizer by checking that it can tear in more than one direction; this will help down the line when you are removing the excess backing from your design. Two, tear the backing as close to the stitching as possible to reduce distortion. This should be done slowly and deliberately to make the tear as clean as possible. And three, avoid using tear-away with delicate or stretchy fabrics, as these are easy to distort or rip in the process of tearing away the backing. It is easy to fall into the habit of just using tear-away, especially if you have accidentally cut your fabric in the past with other types of backing.

Cutaway

This sturdy backing is used for delicate and stretchy fabrics. While you are embroidering or sewing, cutaway backing provides you with a solid foundation, allowing you to make crisp, clean stitches. Cutaway is great for holding the shape of your design on thin fabrics. This means you don't have to deal with angry customers returning with sagging or distorted designs after just a few washes. Just be careful when cutting away the backing, so you do not cut your fabric! Don't cut too close to your stitches, and you should use a gliding motion with your scissors rather than a cutting motion.

Solvy Water Soluble

This type of backing does just as its name suggests – it dissolves in water. It dissolves best in room temperature water. This can be used on the top or underneath your stitching. Use solvy on top of the fabric that is fluffy or has thick loops like towels. This will keep your stitching from getting lost between the fibers, or the loops from poking through your design.

https://www.banaschs.com/three-main-types-of-embroidery-backing/

Blank Garments to Embroider

Though most garments will work fine with embroidery, one word of caution is, on lighter garments, if your embroidery is significant, it will usually weigh down the garment. There might be an outline around

So for this reason, I would recommend avoiding lighter garments or reducing the size of your embroidery.

Understanding Pricing

Variables which Affect Embroidery Pricing:

There can be other variables that affect how much you pay to get your garments decorated and embroidered, but I have found that these 3 variables are the ones that have the most impact on decoration cost.

- **Stitch Count/Sizing**: Embroidery is usually charged by how many stitches are in your design. You find out how many stitches are in your design once you send your design off to be digitized. The bigger your design, the more stitches in your artwork.

- **Location**: Sometimes, embroidery houses can charge you upcharges if your designs are overly too big or if they are in uncommon places that are hard to work with. The main thing to remember here is that the more locations, the more expensive it usually is. Meaning.. front and back are 2 locations so you would pay 2 prices for each location. If possible, keep your

- **Threads**: Just like screenprinting, most embroidery places can't keep in-house every possible thread color for you as it is expensive. Most times, they will have their common and popular colors in house and special order any colors/threads they don't have. These are often referred to as "stock colors or stock threads," you can usually just ask them if there are any special charges for these exact colors. If there is, try sticking to the stock threads.

It's 2020 when I am typing this book, but here is a chart that gives you the pricing from one vendor for how they price their work.

2014 Hat Embroidery Pricing
Pricing Includes 1 Embroidery Location.

	1-7,499 Stitches	7,500 - 14,999 Stitches	15,000+ Stitches
12-35 Hats	$4.00ea	$4.50ea	$5.00ea
36-59 Hats	$3.00ea	$3.50ea	$4.00ea
60-143 Hats	$2.50ea	$3.00ea	$3.50ea
144+ Hats	$2.00ea	$2.50ea	$3.00ea

Advice: How to Get the Best Pricing

My advice to you on getting the best will just be me sharing with you my strategy.

What I like to do is I like to look at the price chart closely. Ideally, producing 1000s of garments will lead to getting you the best possible pricing. However, when you're starting, you might not be able to or want to get 1000s of garments made at once.

So, what I do is I look at the pricing chart closely. I look at which quantity price break has the most savings differential. For example, if you look at the example above, by ordering 60 pcs vs. ordering 12 pcs, you would pay $2.50 per piece instead of $4.00. You notice to get the next price break, and you would have to order 144 pieces. Instead of ordering 60 pieces, if you order 144 pieces, you would only save 50 cents per piece. That is great to get almost 50% off the original MOQ price, but you want to balance your quantity and savings.

This helps you to allocate your capital efficiently and produce where demand is. Remember, dead or slow-moving inventory is the killer for your business and cash flow! Don't get romantic with the inventory.
Focus to Save on Garment Cost

Another thing to remember is, along with being diligent and efficient with getting a great embroidery price, don't overlook your blank garment cost.

One great hack is to order closeouts on RG Riley, as I mentioned earlier. I use these guys a lot for my brands in using closeout inventory.

Finding Decoration Vendors

Before you commit to a vendor for your embroidery, talk to at least 10 people! Get price quotes from all 10 and do some research on the professionalism and attention to detail of the company you're talking to.

I have had horrendous experiences with unprofessional vendors. Unprofessional vendors can be tough to deal with. They change their pricing on you. If they screw up your order or merchandise, they don't bother to make it right, etc.

Not saying everybody is like this, but I have dealt with my fair share of issues with bad apples over the years. It is your money and hard work, and there is nothing wrong with expecting the very best.

Remember, screenprinting and embroidery has relatively low barriers-to-entry so pretty much anyone and their brother can claim that they can get screenprint or embroider for you, but not everyone has the same level of skill or do they even take pride in their work.

Ask to see their portfolio of past work, ask to see samples if you aren't convinced!

Different Type of Embroidery Vendors

There are a few types of vendors that I always try to place each vendor into a bucket.

There are garage / agile printers, which are very agile and flexible with their processes, pricing, etc. They will go above and beyond and work with you and be flexible, but they also struggle with having an established business process. Sometimes, you might pay less or pay more.

There are established / production houses. These guys have been in business for a while, have robust equipment, and can produce without stress. They will usually have an established process and price list. You can expect consistency. However, they rarely will go outside their established procedures, so not really the most flexible, but if their process is good and it works, there is no reason to!

There are also just garbage printers! They don't care about the quality of their work. They don't understand competitive pricing and will tell you a million excuses or their problems. I steer clear of these types of printers.

I like to work with established production houses that have the service level of the agile printers! I have noticed that this blend works the best for me.

FEW MORE PRINTING & MANUFACTURING DECORATION

There are other options that you have when it comes to manufacturing your brand, the ones in this book are the ones which are just what I know and use. Here are some more printing and manufacturing methods which might serve useful for you to know in the back of your mind.

I am not too familiar with these methods but I do want to share briefly what they are and from here, you can do more research on these yourself individually.

Direct-to-Garment:

Direct-to-garment printing (DTG) is a process of printing on textiles using specialized aqueous inkjet technology. DTG printers typically have a platen designed to hold the garment in a fixed position, and the printer inks are jetted or sprayed onto the textile by the print head.

Dye Sublimation:

A dye-sublimation printer is a computer printer that uses heat to transfer dye onto materials such as plastic, card, paper, or fabric. The sublimation name was first applied because the dye was considered to make the transition between the solid and gas states without going through a liquid stage.

Cut & Sew:

The term cut and sew is used to denote a garment that has been customized from raw fabric rather than one that has been purchased from a third-party supplier and then screen-printed or altered.

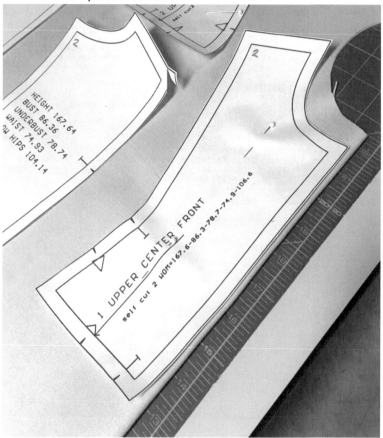

I know that a "tech pack" is something which is an industry term and might be good topic research to find more about creating your own merch with the cut & sew method.

Written By Yaswanth Nukasani ©
www.yaswanthnukasani.com

What is Tech Pack? A tech pack is an informative sheet that designers create to communicate with a manufacturer all the necessary components needed to construct a product. Typically designers will include measurements, materials, colors, trim, hardware, grading, labels, tags, etc.

https://www.thaisonspgarment.com/FAQ/what-is-a-garment-tech-pack.html

"Tech Pack Template"

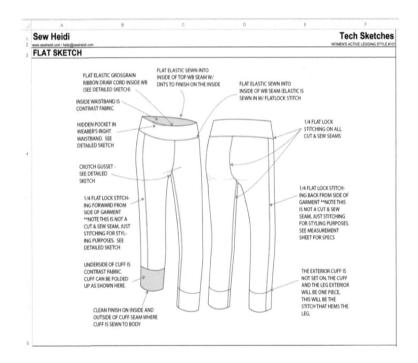

If you want to make your garments from scratch, this is the way to go. I know this is something we want to look into as a brand as we start to scale our business and offer more products.

If you search for cut & sew factories/manufacturers near you, pick up the phone and talk to them and you will pick up a wealth of information.

START YOUR BRAND FOR UNDER $100

So by now, you know about most of the available printing methods and you're knowledgeable, however, if you're struggling to find the funds to launch your brand and get something going. I have one strategy for you which might be the answer.

I personally do not use this strategy mainly because I am able to invest in manufacturing, warehouse, and order fulfillment myself and am able to get a better Return on Investment and grow my brand with more control over the means of production.

However, this is a great way for anyone who wants to launch on a budget, can't figure out the logistics, doesn't want to be super involved with manufacturing, etc.

The strategy is called, Print-on-Demand!

The overview is that you sell your designs/clothing on your own online store using Shopify etc. and then use a third-party fulfillment vendor and they take care of the manufacturing, printing, and shipping of your product directly to your end customer. Pretty much "drop-shipping" custom product to your end customer as if it were you sending it to them.

Shopify explained it perfectly in their article here:

> *Whether you're an artist, writer, designer, or entrepreneur, physical products can be the perfect canvas for monetizing your creativity.*
>
> *From t-shirts to posters, backpacks to books, you can put your own original spin on everyday products and sell them online. However, if you go the traditional route of buying and holding your own inventory, you may be left with a pile of products that aren't selling.*
>
> *Print-on-demand services offer an alternative way to bypass the time, investment, and risk associated with managing inventory, letting you go from creating to selling custom products at a fraction of the cost.*
>
> *Print on demand is a process where you work with a supplier to customize white-label products (like baseball hats or tote bags) with your own designs to sell them on a per-order basis under your own brand.*
>
> *That means you don't pay for the product until after you've actually sold it, so there's no need to buy in bulk or hold any inventory yourself.*
>
> *Plus, with print-on-demand services, everything after the sale, from printing to shipping, is handled by your*

supplier. Once you've set everything up, it takes only a few clicks to fulfill an order once you've made a sale.

You can use print-on-demand services to:

- Test a business idea or new product line for an existing business without the risks that come with buying inventory.
- Monetize an audience you've built. Printing on demand is a great option if you're a YouTuber, cartoonist, or social media influencer who wants to spend your time creating content instead of fulfilling orders.
- Create original products for a niche of customers. For example, apparel for people who are passionate about gaming.
- Easily print one-off items—t-shirts, books, shoes, bags, wall art, phone cases, clocks, laptop skins, mugs, and so much more. You can send these as gifts or keep them for yourself and your team.

The pros and cons of print on demand

Print on demand sites can be used to build a business based on a dropshipping model—where the products and shipping are all handled by a third party. It's one of the most accessible ways to source products or starts an online business, but you should know the perks and limitations before you dive in.

Pros

- Create products quickly: Once you have the design, you can create the product and put it up for sale in minutes.

- *Shipping is taken care of: Shipping and fulfillment are out of your hands and in your supplier's. After the sale, you're just responsible for customer service.*
- *Low investment, lower risk: Since you're not physically holding any inventory, it's easier to add or remove products, test ideas, or pivot your approach.*

Cons

- *Lower margins: Naturally, your costs per item will be higher than if you buy in bulk. On-demand products may yield thinner profits, depending on how you price them and acquire customers.*
- *Less control over shipping: Shipping costs can get complicated as it often varies for different products. Your options may also be limited if you want to create a standout unboxing experience.*
- *Limited customization: Your ability to customize products depends on the vendor and the product. You'll have to weigh base costs, customization options, printing techniques, and available sizes when deciding on which products to customize.*

Source: https://www.shopify.com/blog/print-on-demand

Printful: On-Demand Print & Embroidery Fulfillment:

Create & sell your own custom design products online with print-on-demand drop shipping. Sign up for free and start selling custom product under your own

1	2	3	4
Your online store	Gary from United States	Printful fulfillment center	Your product
Connect your online store with Printful and add your products	Gary buys something on your store	Your order is automatically imported to us for fulfillment	We ship the finished product to Gary, all under your brand

For apparel products, in particular, Printful offers a number of printing techniques. Here are some that you'll want to be aware of:

- Direct to Garment prints ink directly onto the material, which is especially good for simpler designs (i.e. witty t-shirts). You can only print on certain areas of the product as a result.

- Cut and Sew is sometimes known as "all-over print". The article of clothing is printed on in pieces for maximum coverage and then sewn together for a seamless print across the entire piece. While the base costs may be higher, this lets you create a more premium product that you could sell for more.

- Embroidery is perhaps the most complex printing technique because the final product is actually a threaded design with a 3D effect. This is best for simple designs that involve only a handful of colors, and for products like hats that traditionally feature embroidered designs.

You should also be mindful of how additional customizations affect the price. Printing on the sleeve, for example, will usually mean paying a nominal fee on top of the base cost. Besides apparel, Printful also offers mugs, pillows, framed posters, beach towels, aprons, and more.

There are other options like Printify, etc., just search for "print on demand"

Printify simplifies and automates the process of sourcing and creating print-on-demand products at the best prices on the market.

- Pick: Our catalog has over 200 products such as t-shirts, mugs, socks, and home accessories ready for you to customize. Pick the most suitable product for your business based on print provider location, fulfillment time, and price.

- Customize: Use our free Mockup Generator to apply your designs to your chosen products. Easily upload your design, switch between color options, and preview your products on high-quality images. The mockup is designed to easily add products to your online store.

- Sample: Order samples from your chosen print providers to make sure the end products look and feel exactly as you imagined. This allows you to test out different products and find the right print provider for your business.

- Publish: Once you're happy with your custom product, publish it to your online store automatically. Printify is integrated with leading eCommerce platforms such as Shopify, Etsy, eBay, and more so you can sell to millions of online shoppers effortlessly.

- **Relax:** When you make a sale, and your product passes Quality Control, it is sent to production and thereafter, shipped directly to your customer. You can easily track this process from your Printify account. Focus on growing your brand while we take care of the rest.

Source: printify.com

What's notable about Printify is that its international vendor network enables a number of unique white-label products you're not likely to find elsewhere, such as jewelry, clocks, shoes, and water bottles. In fact, the platform boasts over 200 products you can print on.

While Printify is free to use, a premium subscription is available that gives you 20% off of all products for $29 a month, which is a solid option if you're looking to scale up later and improve your profit margins.

There are plenty of options with this, you just have to research it out a little more, I personally think this is a viable option to start but I feel to scale and really grow your brand big you should produce inventory yourself.

PACKAGING

Having a product that people want to buy is great, but success also lies in small things such as packaging in which you deliver your clothing items.

I personally like it when I receive a well-designed branded box and T-shirt nicely folded in the bag that looks like no one touched it before. It gives your customers a special treatment they want and are paying for.

Therefore, you should spend time thinking about what packaging goes best with your clothing line.

When I started, finding the right suppliers was quite difficult, but now below, I have included my recommendations after doing research and testing some options.

POLY BAG

To start, I would recommend you take each garment and place them in a clear 1 mil poly bags. This is not the bags you would ship them in, but rather, these provide protection and easy storage. It avoids things like lint, stains, etc. on your garments while they are in boxes in storage, waiting for the orders to start coming through.

This is what I use, and I found these work well for t-shirts, crewnecks & hoodies

600 Clear ~12x15"
T-Shirt Plastic Bags Self Seal Clothes Apparel Reclosable Poly
11-3/5 x 14-1/8 in-1 mil

For 600 bags, I paid roughly $34. You can find these on eBay. This breaks down to just a few cents per bag. If you are looking for even higher quantity and want to buy in more bulk, you can look at U-Line.

Option #1 Poly Mailer Packaging

Now that you have your garments in clear poly bags, let's talk about packaging when it comes to shipping.

I use Tyvek/polyethylene poly mailers.

This type of packaging is good for clothing startups, as they are very cost-effective. Customers love to feel special.

You don't need to spend a lot of money on thousands of customized packages with your logos printed on the bags etc. If you find that important and your budget allows, you can get custom shipping poly mailers with your own designs/logos and printed on. It would cost thousands of dollars cause you usually have to order 1000s for it to be cost-effective.

The best thing about Poly mailers is that you can buy them blank and customize them as you want.

You can also find poly mailers which already have designs printed on them. For example, for my brand, we use "pineapple poly mailers." Depending on your brand theme, you can find designs that are a better fit, "cactus poly mailers," "tie-dye poly mailers," etc.

I bought 200 tie-dye designer poly mailers for $20.13 on eBay.

200 10x13 Tie Dye Designer Mailers Poly Shipping Envelopes Boutique Bags

If you don't find any poly mailers with designs you like, you can buy stickers with your logo that you can quickly slap onto the poly mailers.

If you get lucky, you can find designs that match your brand aesthetic already printed so you will reduce your costs even more, as I mentioned earlier.

These poly mailers are flexible and don't tear as they are usually made of a material called Tyvek that lasts, ensuring your product is delivered safely.

That said, the benefits of Poly mailers are:

- *Cost-effective*: You can go on Amazon and buy thousands of them for very little money.
- *Low-upfront cost*: It is possible to order 100-200 bags for just $20-$30.
- *Easy to customize*: You can add your stickers. Available in many colors and styles. They allow you to try so many different colorful designs.

2. Box Mailer packaging

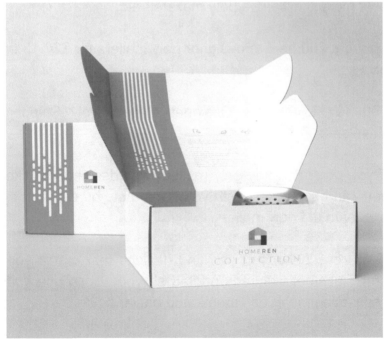

Written By Yaswanth Nukasani ©
www.yaswanthnukasani.com

By using boxes, your product will look more classy, earn a better reputation, and make your buyers appreciate it more.

Well-branded clothing business is always taken seriously, allowing you to play with prices a bit more. You might have seen these cardboard box mailers, which a lot of subscription businesses use.

- **Very professional look.** (If you have an iPhone, you might still be saving its box somewhere in your room.)

- **High- upfront cost:** They look better, but they also cost more.

- **Easy to customize** - Buy a rubber stamp and make your own.

One company that we use for packaging is Paper Mart. They have different types of packaging so that you can pick your favorite. You can enjoy multiple designs, even ones made from wood.

Make sure to avoid ordering 10 different sizes as you will have to invest more, rather buy 1-2 sizes which will fit most of your orders and garments when you ship them.

PaperMart usually is a lot cheaper than the ones you will find on Amazon. The main disadvantage of PaperMart is that you can only buy them in the bulk of 50 to 100. They also have smaller bulks, but they come at a higher price.

One good hack is, you can buy multiple color tissues to stuff your boxes/bags with as it will look like a personalized gift rather than a boring delivery.

Our second packaging supplier is Uline. They also have different types of mailers.

Uline is a bit more expensive upfront than Paper Mart. Think about it like Costco; spend more upfront, but your dollar goes farther.

They offer more unique designs, so they are good when you need something specific. Also, like any other wholesale, the more you buy, the better deal you will get to save some money. So, make an order carefully while calculating what the best for you is.

I would recommend you buy some on eBay when you're starting off, and if you're starting to get a high volume of orders, then transition to a true wholesaler like U-Line.

Finishing Touches on Your Garments

Now that you have an idea on the packaging, the next thing to consider is the finishing touches to put it all together.

Fold: Make sure to fold your shirts/hoodies etc. nicely before you place them into your clear poly bags for storage.

Hang Tag: A hang tag is usually like the price tag or the tag with your brand logo on them. You might have seen this if you have bought any clothing item in the store.

Option #1

You can get them printed in bulk with your own custom logos professionally. I usually
Use GotPrint for hang tags like this.

Option #2

You can also buy cardstock paper, design them on a software like Microsoft Word, Adobe Illustrator, print them on cardstock paper and cut them out. If you search "DIY hangtag," you will find many videos that show you how to do this.

You have to punch a little hole in them to put the string through so you can attach it to your shirt.

Once you have your hang tags, you need to find a way to attach them to your garment.

You have two options here. I recommend that you use Hang Tag fasteners as it just looks more "premium." The cost is not much more.

- Hang Tag Fasteners Gold Safety Pin - 1000 pieces - $18.05 for all of them (eBay)
- Regular Clothing Price Label Tagging Tag tagger Gun With 1000 3" Barbs+1 Needle - $8 (eBay)

You will usually have to pierce a hole in the garment to attach your hang tag to the garment. I recommend piercing the neck label tag or right under the arm-pit area of the sleeve.

Stickers:

Another nice thing to do is get your own stickers made or just some cool stickers which you can include for your customers so that they can place them on their laptop, phone, etc.

Custom Stickers: allstickerprinting.com
Bulk Cool Stickers: aliexpress.com → search for "cool vinyl stickers," etc.

You can buy 100 pretty cool pop culture stickers for $3 with free shipping.
Size Stickers: Having a size sticker label on the clear poly bag which your garment is in is not a complete necessity, but it can help you distinguish the size of the garment when it is inside the polybag, and you can't see the neck label.

You can get as creative as you want.

I have even thought about putting things like these in packages just to create an extremely memorable experience for our customers.

- Candy/Mints
- Little bits of car air fresheners (for example my brand is all about pineapples so maybe a package which smells like pineapples)
- Marbles
- Baseball Cards
- Goody bag type of stuff (stuff which you find in goody bags)
- Stickers
- _____ < your idea here...

SALES & MARKETING GUIDE FOR CLOTHING BRANDS

To finalize your clothing business set up, you will need to decide how you are going to promote them. In this part, I will share the best techniques I used to develop my profitable clothing business.

The key is to have the right tools for the job so you can have effects on your marketing.

The tips & tools that are great techniques which will help you increase your clothing business chances for success are as follows:

1. Set Up an E-commerce Website

Though it is still very viable to try and sell your clothing brand to boutique stores and retailers, having an online store and going directly to consumers is something which is relatively easy and powerful.

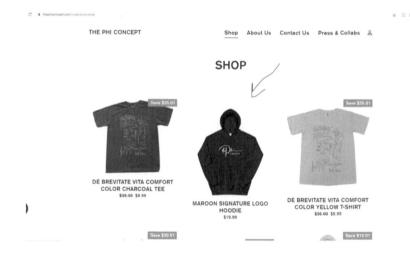

You need an e-commerce store for your clothing brand. You can set up your online store using Shopify. It is extremely user friendly, allowing you to navigate through your website easily even though you might not be an experienced developer.

With a few clicks, you can add pages such as a blog or gallery and make your e-commerce website more attractive to your viewers.

I checked many similar services, but Shopify remained the best. Its dashboard provides many tools you need for your business.

For example, you have a handy analytics option that informs you about your sales and costs so you can create more exact plans for the future.

You can also see your conversion rate that signals how many visitors decided to buy something from you to measure your marketing success.

For $29 per month, you can have your own eCommerce website.

There are other services such as WooCommerce that can be integrated into your WordPress website. But it is not easy to navigate as you can with Shopify. Shopify has a great app store with a bunch of free tools you can use

2. Create Your Online Stores on Other Platforms

Nowadays if you want to maximize your e-commerce earnings, especially clothing business revenue, you shouldn't miss a chance to sell your products on Amazon and Etsy.

Written By Yaswanth Nukasani ©
www.yaswanthnukasani.com

Amazon is the largest marketplace that operates on a global scale. You might have heard about it, but it is easy to buy something from there, however, not to sell. There are two types of

Amazon accounts, individual and professional. You might want to consider opening an individual one as the business one costs $39.99 per month.

Aside from that, there are seller fees that include $0.99 per item, referral fees. And variable closing fees. But when you start gaining significant earnings, this won't be much. Make sure to do your research and learn about each platform's process.

Etsy is also an online marketplace, but the one that is more cost-effective in the beginning as it costs only $10 per month or even for free.

You can sell everything from designs to digital downloads that are becoming very popular these days as they can create you an amazing side income even while you are sleeping.

Setting up an Etsy store is a great way to push your brand name in the search engines as it partnered with Google by linking Google Shopping to its platform.

eBay is a bit different seller model, which also has customers from all over the world. It functions as both a fixed price and auction-based system where you are charged 9% of the price for the items you sell.

3.Start Email Campaigns

After you have set up stores and started getting customer information, it will be wise to use it with other tools to optimize your customer engagement and sales. You can start by creating a Mail Chimp account where you can run multiple email campaigns such as welcoming new customers or trying to reach new ones by sending cold email sequences.

There you also have the analytics tool that helps you track how many people have opened your email or how many reacted to it by subscribing to your store.

4. Set Up Social Media Pages to Get More Fans

Social Media Marketing is huge. I am sure you have heard this before, but if you know what you are doing, there are brands that completely just blow up just from Instagram.

You are not reaching your sales potential if you don't have an online presence and especially social media.

There are more than 3 billion users on social media platforms...

Social media channels have become the 21st-century shopping malls where you can hang out but also buy from your favorite stores.

That is why businesses aim to be there.

Facebook, Instagram, and Twitter are the best platforms to start promoting your clothing business.

Make sure to have matching information and visuals on all these pages. Knowing how to write engaging sales and marketing copy will definitely make a difference.

You can link your Instagram to your Facebook account and promote all three pages in your email campaigns, getting the best of all of them.

Besides your creativity, to develop your ad message and overall content for your marketing campaigns, you can use tools such as Canva and Pexels. Both will provide you with the graphics you need.

With Canva, you can create social media posts.

Pexels will provide you with all the types of images and videos that will help you tell your story and increase your content production value.

The best thing about these two tools is that they are both free.

You can just follow these steps, and your rewards will come, slowly but surely!

Written By Yaswanth Nukasani ©
www.yaswanthnukasani.com

Closing Remarks

I hope this book has been useful to you. I truly believe I have included the required information for you to get your brand started.

I am sure there will be remaining questions, but it is all a continuous learning process, and together, we will figure it out as we go! Keep your eye out for some new books which I already have some book ideas for!

Feel free to write to me at peter.nukasani@gmail.com or send me a message on Instagram @yaswanthnukasani

I will do my best to help you in any way I can. Look forward to hearing from you, and I hope to hear about your brand on the big screens in the near future.

From our brand, apparel printing company, and me, I wish you the best of luck and will be here for you in your journey and I salute you in your journey.

With Love,
Yaswanth Nukasani

Few Pics Over the Years from our journey of building our clothing brand, the Phi Concept...

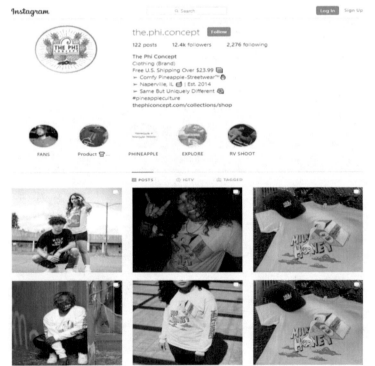

Written By Yaswanth Nukasani ©
www.yaswanthnukasani.com

Who is this book for?

This book is for anyone that wants to start a brand or learn how to get run of t-shirts printed for a great price.

This book does not take forever to finish! I have made this book as short as possible and packed in as much information I could. This book should take a couple of hours to read, but you will most likely have to wait a week or two for your shirts to be printed!

In the meantime, you will learn how to get a design and logo made for $5 from professional designers, source wholesale blank apparel, and get the best pricing on screen printing these shirts.

You will also learn the optimal and most powerful way to set up an online store, launch your marketing

You will walk away from this book with super high quality and a fair priced batch of shirts on the way, basic knowledge on how screenprinting and embroidery work, and an online store that is all set up and ready to bring in sales!

The most valuable skill as an entrepreneur is sales & marketing. We have developed the ultimate cheat sheet when it comes to learning how to manufacture, sell, and scale your clothing brand.

What is in it for you?

- You will avoid all the mistakes I made when starting my brand
- You will learn step by step the process of sourcing your product and selling it online
- You will get your brand up and running
- You will skip the usual mistakes, and avoid wasting money when getting started